THE

RESPONSIBILITY OF THE NORTH

IN RELATION TO

SLAVERY.

CAMBRIDGE:
PRINTED BY ALLEN AND FARNHAM.
1856.

THE RESPONSIBILITY OF THE NORTH IN RELATION TO SLAVERY.

During a debate near the close of the last session of Congress, it was asserted that if the New England States had voted in the convention for forming the constitution, against the extension of the slave-trade, it would have been abolished eight years sooner than it was, and charging it upon Massachusetts that, on account of her interest in the slave-trade, her members voted in favor of continuing it until 1808. On some doubt being expressed as to the correctness of this charge, a southern member challenged a contradiction, and one of the Massachusetts senators was ready to confess for his constituents, for the sake of saying that they had since repented. All this seemed to be a new discovery, and I was at a loss to know on what authority it was founded. Upon examination I find it depends upon an article published in the National Intelligencer, quoting from the journal of the convention as follows: — "The first committee on the subject consisted of Rutledge of South Carolina, Randolph of Virginia, Wilson of Pennsylvania, Gorham of Massachusetts, and Ellsworth of Connecticut, and they reported as a section for the constitution, 'That no tax or other duty should be laid on the migration or importation of such persons as the several States should think proper to admit, nor shall such migration or importation be prohibited.'

"This was the first action of the convention on the slavery question; and it will be seen that a committee, the majority of which was from what are now strong anti-slavery States, reported against any future prohibition of the African slave-trade, but were willing to legalize it perpetually.

"This section was subsequently referred to a committee selected by ballot, consisting of Langdon of New Hampshire, King of Massachusetts, Johnson of Connecticut, Livingston of New Jersey, Clymer of Pennsylvania, Dickinson of Delaware, Martin of Maryland, Madison of Virginia, Williamson of North Carolina, C. C. Pinckney of South Carolina, and Baldwin of Georgia. This committee, a majority of which was from *slave* States, reported the clause with authority to Congress to prohibit the slave-trade after the year 1800, and in the mean time to levy a tax on such importations. This section was afterwards modified and adopted as it now exists in the constitution, extending the time before which Congress could not prohibit the trade until 1808; Massachusetts, New Hampshire, and Connecticut, *free States*, and Maryland, North and South Carolina, *slave States*, voting for the extension, New Jersey and Pennsylvania, *free States*, and Delaware and Virginia, *slave States*, voting against it." So far the statement in the Intelligencer.

The inferences drawn are as follows: —

"1. A committee, the majority of which was from

free States, report in favor of denying to Congress the power at any period to prohibit the African slave-trade."

"2. That a subsequent committee, a majority of which was from the *slave* States, reported a new section, authorizing Congress to abolish the trade after 1800."

"3. That this period was extended until the year 1808, thus giving eight additional years to the traffic, by the vote of New Hampshire, Massachusetts, and Connecticut, while the vote of Virginia was against such extension."

All this bears such an appearance of authenticity, that we are not surprised that it has found its way into Mr. Adams's "South side View of Slavery," — but he goes somewhat further, and makes New England responsible for the slaves imported between 1800 and 1808, with all their posterity, estimated at 300,000, and asks, "Can any one inform us where Northern moral sense was, or whether it was in the convention, when the North protracted the slave-trade eight years longer than the South wished to endure it?"

Before this becomes settled as an uncontradicted charge against New England, it may be well to examine the matter a little further, which we are fortunately able to do by the "Debates in the Federal Convention," published in the "Madison Papers,"* and we shall find that the whole proceedings give no warrant, either for the charge that Massachusetts was influenced in her

* The report of Judge Yates contains nothing on the subject, he having left the convention on the 5th of July, before this matter came under consideration.

votes by the interest of her citizens in the slave-trade, or that the North protracted the slave-trade *eight years longer than the South wished to endure it.*

The history of the proceedings of the convention is as follows. From their organization on the 25th of May, 1787, to the 26th of July, the convention was engaged in discussing and deciding on the principles which should be embodied in the constitution, and on the various plans and motions which were submitted for their consideration. Having decided, in a preliminary manner, upon most of these, in the form of resolutions, on Monday, July 23d, it was voted, "That the *proceedings of the convention* for the establishment of a national government be referred to a committee to prepare and report a constitution *conformable thereto.*"

This committee was appointed by ballot on the 24th, consisting of Messrs. Rutledge, Randolph, Gorham, Ellsworth, and Wilson, who are afterwards several times referred to as the "*committee of detail.*" And on "the 26th, the proceedings since Monday last were unanimously referred to the *committee of detail,* and the convention unanimously adjourned till Monday, August 6th, that the *committee of detail* might have time to prepare and report the constitution."

It may be well to notice here, how carefully the authority of this committee is restricted. Though the vote was passed on the 23d of July referring the *proceedings of the convention* to the committee, to prepare and report a constitution *conformable thereto,* the convention still proceed until the 26th to debate and settle further principles, and then refer these further proceedings to the same committee for the same purpose, after having completed what may be considered their instructions to the committee. This *committee of detail* is the first committee alluded to in the article from the Intelligencer, a majority of which was from the free States, and who are charged with reporting the article against any future prohibition of the African slave-trade. Now it will be seen that the duty of this committee was only to digest and prepare a constitution *in conformity with the proceedings already taken by the convention.* In reporting the preliminary form of a constitution, containing the article above mentioned, they could only be responsible for the faithful digest and arrangement of the proceedings of the convention referred to them for this purpose, and in obeying the instructions of the convention they should be fairly and fully exonerated on their part from the guilt of any intention of "legalizing slavery perpetually."

It should be further mentioned as an indication of the prevailing feeling at the time, that on the passage of the vote for this committee, "General Pinckney reminded the convention that if the committee should fail to insert some security to the Southern States against an emancipation of slaves, and taxes on exports, he should be bound by duty to his State to vote against their report." *

Having now disposed of the first accusation against the North, and seen how far the committee from the *free States* are chargeable with a disposition to "*legalize slavery*," it is time to proceed to an examination of the further doings of the convention.

* Madison Papers, p. 1187.

The *committee of detail* reported the proposed form and outline of a constitution on the 6th of August, containing the article as first drawn respecting slavery, with the clause denying to Congress the power to prohibit the importation of slaves, and the convention then proceeded to debate and decide upon the several articles, with or without amendment. On Tuesday, the 21st day of August, as appears by the journal of the convention, when this part of the report was under consideration, "on the question to agree to the first clause of the fourth section of the seventh article as reported, it passed in the affirmative. It was then moved and seconded to insert the word '*free*' before '*persons*' in the fourth section of the seventh article. The clause would then read, 'No tax or duty shall be laid by the legislature on articles exported from any State, nor on the migration or importation of such *free persons* as the several States shall think proper to admit, nor shall such migration be prohibited.'" A debate on this motion was continued until the adjournment for the day, and part of the next day, during which, the journal says, the motion was withdrawn, and it appears from the language used by some of the speakers that a motion was under consideration to strike out the clause.

A few extracts from the speeches of the members will show the feelings of the North and of the South on the subject of slavery, and enable the reader to decide how far the North was guilty of protracting the slave-trade "eight years longer than the South wished to endure it."

When that part of the report relating to representation in Congress was under consideration, Mr. King, of

Massachusetts, had remarked that "the admission of slaves was a most grating circumstance to his mind, and he believed would be so to a great part of the people of America. He had not made a strenuous opposition to it heretofore, because he had hoped that this concession would have produced a readiness, which has not been manifested, to strengthen the general government, and to mark a full confidence in it. The report under consideration had, by the tenor of it, put an end to all these hopes. In two great points the hands of the legislature were absolutely tied. The importation of slaves could not be prohibited. Exports could not be taxed. . . . . He had hoped that some accommodation would have taken place on the subject, that at least a time would have been limited for the importation of slaves. He never could agree to let them be imported without limitation, and then to be represented in the national legislature." On the same occasion Gouverneur Morris of Pennsylvania said, "He never could concur in upholding domestic slavery. It was a most nefarious institution, it was the curse of heaven on the States where it prevailed." *

On the 21st of August, in the debate upon the article respecting the importation of slaves, Mr. Rutledge of South Carolina said, — "The true question at present is whether the Southern States shall or shall not be parties to the Union."

Mr. C. C. Pinckney of South Carolina said, "South Carolina can never receive the plan if it prohibits the slave-trade. In every proposed extension of the power

* Madison Papers, p. 1261–1263.

of Congress that State has expressly and watchfully excepted that of meddling with the importation of negroes."*

General Pinckney of South Carolina "declared it to be his firm opinion that if himself and all his colleagues were to sign the constitution and use their personal influence, it would be of no avail towards obtaining the consent of their constituents. South Carolina and Georgia cannot do without slaves . . . . should consider a rejection of the clause as an exclusion of South Carolina from the Union."

Mr. Dickinson of Delaware "considered it as inadmissible on every principle of honor and safety that the importation of slaves should be authorized to the States by the constitution."

Mr. Williamson of North Carolina "thought the Southern States could not be members of the Union if the clause should be rejected."

Mr. King of Massachusetts "thought the subject should be considered in a political light only. If two States will not agree to the constitution, as stated on one side, he could affirm with equal belief on the other, that great and equal opposition would be experienced from other States."

Mr. Langdon of New Hampshire was strenuous for giving the power to the general government. He could not, with a good conscience, leave it with the States, who could then go on with the traffic."†

General Pinckney of South Carolina "thought himself bound to declare candidly that he did not think South

* Madison Papers, p. 1389–1392. † Ib. p. 1394, 1395.

Carolina would stop her importation of slaves in any short time; but only stop them occasionally as she now does." He moved that the clause be committed, evidently for the purpose of so modifying the article as to permit the importation.

Mr. Rutledge of South Carolina said, "If the convention thinks that North Carolina, South Carolina, and Georgia will ever agree to the plan, unless their right to import slaves be untouched, the expectation is vain. The people of those States will never be such fools as to give up so important an interest. He was strenuous against striking out the section, and seconded the motion of Gen. Pinckney for a commitment." *

Mr. Sherman of Connecticut said "it was better to let the Southern States import slaves than to part with them, if they made that a *sine quâ non.*"

Mr. Randolph of Virginia was "for committing in order that some middle ground might, if possible, be found. He could never agree to the clause as it stands. He would sooner risk the constitution." †

Mr. Ellsworth of Connecticut said, "If we do not agree upon this middle and moderate course he was afraid we should lose two States, with such others as may be disposed to stand aloof, should fly into a variety of shapes and directions, and most probably into several confederations, and not without bloodshed." ‡

Thus after a protracted and warm discussion, it became evident that some compromise must be effected to reconcile the conflicting views of the North and the South; and on motion of General Pinckney of South

* Madison Papers, p. 1395, 1396. † Ib. p. 1396, 1397.
‡ Ib. p. 1397.

Carolina, seconded by Mr. Rutledge of the same State, the subject was referred to a committee of one from each State then represented in the convention, evidently to find some "middle ground" as suggested by Mr. Randolph of Virginia, and assented to by Mr. Ellsworth and Mr. Sherman of Connecticut, rather than lose some of the Southern States, and at the hazard of "flying off into several confederations."

This committee of eleven was appointed on the 22d of August, consisting of Mr. Langdon of New Hampshire, Mr. King of Massachusetts, Mr. Johnson of Connecticut, Mr. Livingston of New Jersey, Mr. Clymer of Pennsylvania, Mr. Dickinson of Delaware, Mr. Martin of Maryland, Mr. Madison of Virginia, Mr. Williamson of North Carolina, Mr. C. C. Pinckney of South Carolina, and Mr. Baldwin of Georgia. On the 24th of August this committee reported the clause in the following form. "The migration or importation of such persons as the several States now existing shall think proper to admit, shall not be prohibited by the legislature, prior to the year 1800."

In the foregoing debates we see no want of zeal in favor of the slave-trade, on the part of the South, and no indifference on the part of the North with regard to the slave-trade, or slavery in general. But it became very evident, that, in order to keep the States together, there must be some compromise upon the subject, and the committee of eleven was chosen for this purpose. The South insisted that Congress should have no power to impose any restrictions on the importation of slaves, and the North was determined that there must be a restriction or prohibition in future, if not at present. The result was a report from the committee, in substance allowing Congress the power of prohibiting the slave-trade after the year 1800, and restricting them from the exercise of that power before that time. But the terms of this compromise were not satisfactory to the South, and on the 25th of August, when the report came under consideration, it was amended by inserting 1808 instead of 1800. From the fact that this amendment was made without debate, and upon the motion of Gen. Pinckney from the South, seconded by Mr. Gorham from the North, and that the report was not acted upon until the next day after it was laid before the convention, it may fairly be presumed that, in the mean time, the contending parties had come to an understanding upon the subject, and agreed to settle it by a silent vote. But there is no indication of any change of opinion or feeling, either by northern or southern members, from what had been expressed in the preceding debate. Even after the question was decided, "Gouverneur Morris was for making the clause read at once, '*The importation of slaves into North Carolina, South Carolina, and Georgia shall not be prohibited,*' etc. This, he said, would be most fair. . . . . He wished it to be known that this part of the constitution was a compliance with those States. If the change of language, however, should be objected to by the members from those States, he should not urge it."*

That the same feeling continued to prevail with the southern members is evident from the course taken by Mr. Rutledge of South Carolina within a week of the

* Madison Papers, p. 1427.

close of the convention. When the provisions respecting amendments to the constitution were under consideration, with true southern perseverance, to guard against every possibility of defeat where the interest of his State was concerned, he said, "He never would agree to give a power by which the articles relating to slaves might be altered by the States not interested in that property, and prejudiced against it." In order to obviate this objection these words were added to the proposition:—"Provided that no amendments which may be made prior to the year 1808, shall in any manner affect the fourth and fifth sections of the seventh article."*

Now let us look back to the view of the case with which we commenced, and which amounts to little less than a charge upon the free States as the advocates of slavery, and giving the slave States the credit of being the champions of freedom. One would think that the absurdity of this would secure it from currency and belief, but nothing seems too absurd to gain credit with those who are disposed to believe a thing because it is unreasonable. Published in a widely circulating paper at the seat of government, with some show of authority by quotation from the journal of the convention, adopted as correct in a work professing to take a candid view of the matter, quoted and repeated by southern men in their speeches in the senate, uncontradicted,—nay, admitted by a senator from the North, what should prevent it from becoming a settled axiom of history,—such as might well give occasion for the remark of Wal-

* Madison Papers, p. 1536.

pole, "Give me any thing but history, for that *must* be false." To be sure the materials exist for correcting the falsehood; but what influence have such materials, resting upon the shelves of our libraries, against the confident assertions of political writers upon an exciting subject, constantly obtruded before the public by a party press.

From the whole of the foregoing view of the matter there seems to be no reason to charge any northern State or individual with lukewarmness in regard to slavery, or to compliment the South with any excess of liberality on the subject. Without indulging in any animosity or reproaches against the North or the South, it is very clear that the articles of the constitution in relation to slavery, as well as many other subjects, were the result of concession and compromise, without which it would have been impossible to have agreed upon the constitution under which we have thus far prospered, or to have devised any means of continuing that *union of States* which has made us a *nation*, and without which we should only have been a weak confederacy, or perhaps a league of contending communities. It is much to be regretted that there is at present such a want of that conciliatory feeling, the true "*spirit of 'seventy-six*," as must make us doubt whether, even in this age of improvement, we are in reality growing wiser than our fathers.

CAMBRIDGE, March, 1856.

www.ingramcontent.com/pod-product-compliance
Lightning Source LLC
LaVergne TN
LVHW010834120826
845149LV00016B/1372

* 9 7 8 1 4 1 8 1 9 0 2 3 1 *